Philadelphia Flowers

Poems by

Roberta Hill Whiteman

Philadelphia Flowers

Poems by

Roberta Hill Whiteman

Holy Cow! Press · Duluth, Minnesota · 1996

I wish to acknowledge and thank the editors of the following publications where
some of the poems in this collection first appeared:

*Abraxis, Amicus Journal, An Ear To The Ground: An Anthology of Contemporary Amer-
ican Poetry, The Chariton Review, Common Ground: A Gathering of Poems on Rural
Life, Early Ripening, Farm Women on the Prairie Frontier, Harper's Anthology of Twen-
tieth Century Native American Poetry, Kali-wesaks, North American Review, Tamaqua,
Upriver Three, Wisconsin Academy Review, Wisconsin Dialogue, Words in the Blood.*

The title poem "Philadelphia Flowers" was commissioned and aired on Minnesota
Public Radio's program, "Presidential Choices" in 1992.

I also wish to acknowledge and thank the following for their awards and grants which
enabled me to complete this collection: *The Lila Wallace-Reader's Digest Fund, The
Jerome Foundation, The College of Physicians and Surgeons of Philadelphia, The Dr.
L. Rosa Minoka-Hill Fund,* and *The University of Wisconsin.*

Library of Congress Cataloging-in-Publication Data

Whiteman, Roberta Hill.
    Philadelphia flowers : poems / by Roberta Hill Whiteman.
       p.   cm.
    ISBN 0-930100-64-6 (pbk.)
     1. Oneida Indians — Poetry.   I. Title
PS3573.H4875P45   1995
811' .54—dc20   95-23057
                                                   CIP

Publisher's Address:

Holy Cow! Press
Post Office Box 3170
Mount Royal Station
Duluth, Minnesota 55803

This project is supported, in part, by a grant from the National Endowment for
the Arts in Washington, D.C., from the Arrowhead Regional Arts Council through
an appropriation from the Minnesota State Legislature, and by generous individuals.

for

Jacob, Heather and Melissa

TABLE OF CONTENTS

ONE

TWO

A person brought to death by grief
cannot see the sky
cannot hear bird song or children's voices
A person brought to death by grief
cannot breathe and speak
cannot feel the sun
A person brought to death by grief
lives stooped by heartache
in a house where firebrands lie scattered

The One Who Holds The Heavens Up
who sends us dreams and life
has given us the gift of words
to bring comfort and care
to recall for the grieving
the beauty of this peaceful place
the beauty in our continuance

—inspired by reading "The Traditional History of the Confederacy of
the Six Nations," recorded at Ohswekan Council House, August 17,
1900, recorded in *The Transactions of the Royal Society of Canada*, 1911.

KOLANCHOE

Your stems rise quietly,
not quivering from touch,
but from memory forced
to send beyond its pain
a brighter thing. Alive
with light, your leaves contain
the waves of an early world,
a shoal lapping up the shadow
of itself. I am charmed
whenever you are there,
calling without a tongue,
turning my living room
into a warehouse
of skittery reflections.

Heal me, lovely, burning
so green, like jade stones
the old ones placed in the mouths
of their dead, sending them
ahead of the harvest,
their spirits, rising stars.
In euphoria, I flaunted
a thousand faces,
unraveled alibis, denied
your richer world until today,
when, like a bowline knot,
this winter glare held me
in the small country of my life.
Like a woman rescued
from a glacier, who can't
completely understand

what death she left behind,
I hear the white wind still
working chasms, the crows,
raucous in the blow,
and sometimes, in a fragile moment,
rivers humming deep below.
Startled by your leaves,
I could no longer rave,
for you smelled like a tropical
mountain and praised the kind orbit
of earth with the open mirth
of your flowers.
You saved me from myself.

I've been afraid of my flowering,
afraid to send from this spinning
dark the little lights
in eyes that laugh.
Disciplined by a pot
and the pinch of my thumb,
you create clusters
of evening clouds, always moving
beyond me. Ah, your old leaves,
stippled with blood,
fold like human hands,
while a few of your flowers
shrivel into moths,
so silver in their slumber,
the new moon will envy them.

DREAMING IN BROAD DAYLIGHT

Rising in the quiet dark, the morning star takes
the torturous errors of this haunted world
and changes them to wings. My adolescence clings

like a burr against my heart. In this life,
we walk a spiral way and must return
to that ecstacy burning in our youth.

Sometimes when you stand in the corridor
of my dreams, your black eyes awaken
forgotten rhythms in my blood.

I long to escape to the sea, for only
the hiss, the crash of surf can stop my dreaming
in broad daylight. I see the roof collapse.

The wind breaks through the rafters,
but you, steady as a boulder in the ruins,
continue to make me bloom amid destruction.

You are a gargoyle, a guardian from far south,
who keeps me from despair in this year
when we rekindle the fire of compassion.

We live on separate levels and never touch,
yet I must suffer the lightning you bring
when you point to a gap in the roof

from which we watch the precession of stars.
In a time before time took you, I felt
your leaving. Not in your gait, nor those black eyes,

but in your smile and ready laugh, death relayed
an ancient message. Was your loneliness the length
of mountain road where they beat you to a grave?

Now when I wake, though I never wake completely,
some of that same grace drives me toward compassion.
I see it in the trees, glistening deep green in half-dark.

Our lives linger on the outer edge of night
from where such knowledge comes. Birds flutter and sing,
as the morning star spills wind across our world.

FIRST LANGUAGE

My fingers worked hard to move
red and purple beads along a wire
while mother pushed me
in a blue stroller down a street
so wide, so full of light,
I wanted to keep the name for yellow
on that morning. She turned from the regular
jolts of the sidewalk
to shove me along a cobblestone path.
In that green canyon, I feel my voice
thrumming ahhhh into air.
The stroller stops. She is no longer there.

Beings on great green legs loom
above me. Their sapphire, scarlet and lemon arms
whirl with such radiance
my toes tingle. Crowded, they bobble
about me, but my hat, both a frame and shade,
protects me from their intense glances.
Sunlight drips like syrup
down my back. When I look up,
the great dish with yellow rays
murmurs in a vibrant voice
above the sudden brush of a breeze.

Filling myself again with sound, I answer,
dew sparkling on grass and green
around me. Drifting through my daily life,
I'm blanketed by this memory bordering on dream.
The ruby hum of that conversation
makes me listen when earth awakens

her green beings, and they begin to speak
our first language of motion and color
and connection. One of the dispossessed,
I took from the sunflower a talisman,
one striped seed remains
locked in the cave of my soul
to remind me both silence
and song belong to the earth.

WHERE I COME FROM

*Even native peoples who have been here 25,000 years were probably
immigrants from Asia.* —Lucy R. Lippard

Intricate energies of our roots on Turtle Island
have supported us. It's difficult to accept
how long we've been here. In the pulse
of my daily life, ancient spirits send

sunlight winking through leaves.
With horns of wisdom and feathered arms,
they travel swiftly, dazzle me and lift
my sorrow. Intimate with this earth,

we pay attention. In wind blasting treetops
before the first summer rain, in the night sky
wide with stars and from those images ancestors
pecked into cliffs and onto stones,

these spirits come to quicken us with a presence
as unsettling as mountain shadows.
I come from the red earth of Turtle Island.
This earth has always been our home.

My ancestors were not immigrants from Asia.
Twenty-five thousand years ago, they
didn't trudge over the MacKensie Corridor
in search of more wooly mammoths.

The one who gives us life, mind, and blood
has enclosed his vision and breath in our bodies,
so we might add to this beauty.
We were not created to atone

for some long ago mistake.
We were not made to beg from another's bowl,
or to control the ancient energies of earth.
The one whose beauty drifts in clouds,

whose voice rises from the thrush
in its tangle of brambles,
whose power attracts us to the sigh
and surge of the sea, asked that we

add to this beauty and be grateful for each day.
We are glad we still remember
how to make with our hands, our eyes, our voices,
these forms, these visions, these songs.

WHAT SHE NAMED HIM

for Darlene

Shishaywin, Breath of God,
sleeps with ten days of new life curled
in his tight fists,
his arms still coated
with birthing down,
his left arm stretched over him
a little moan.
He peers at mother's dress,
the turquoise of a still familiar sky.
God blows up new leaves outside the window.
The willow prepares her summer whispers.

In his blanket of pink cats and blue zebras,
he grunts and flushes,
feeling himself swimming the sea
to her arms, squinting when he feels again
the dust God blew into his eyes
as he emerged.
Our wisdom must be earth-won.

He will be an orator.
Already he raises his left arm for silence.
His face composed as a poppy.
His mouth oh-oh in astonishment
of what comes—butterfly, stone,
turtle, shoe, mushroom, star, toes.
The roaring train startles his afternoon.
Sucking four fingers at a time,

he dreams of poling a tule boat
under dense purple shadows,
the glowing reeds an envelope
of greens, indigo, soft yellow,
while the unseen breath of God
flattens cumulus, fosters
hair he'll find in another month.

What can we give him?
This new world.
White flags of strawberries
signal its coming. Already our adolescent
sun has juggled greater
configurations of stars.

Breath of God, *Sheshaywin,*
smiles at the wall, then bleats
at his new world. He plans to tell jokes,
to travel south, to offer his mother
heartache and joy
at the same moment,
one in each hand.

WATERFALL AT COMO PARK

She's always walking off the edge,
allowing the wellspring of herself
to fall away without worry.

Even in a furious wind, she's out there,
shaking her glinting spray across the sandstone.
Through thick August afternoons,

she gazes at the sky and stays
poised enough to welcome sparrows.
Both structure and flux, she trembles

as she collects pebbles and leaves, while
her basin grows deeper, more substantial.
Those days when love is distant,

I return to her and learn how she sinks,
climbs and leaps into abundant moments
where she gives without purpose

or boundary. She teaches me to believe
in this—it's best we're blind
to that which moving, moves us.

In her great-hearted leaps, she's my anchor,
gathering shadow and sun
without once stopping her song.

ACKNOWLEDGMENT

"I fight so they will recognize me and treat me like a human being."
—Rigoberto Menchu

Listen, for the Lord
of the Near and Close comes
to make you see
in steam rising from coffee,
smoke from bodies burning in Panzos.
Sometime he'll have you taste
in your chocolate bars
that bitterness children carry
when they dare not bury
their bludgeoned mothers.

On the backs of owls,
Izquic, Woman's Blood, flew
out of smoldering hells,
carrying within her twins
who restored freedom
to those sunlit mountains.
Sometime she'll have you smell
in the red and fragrant flowers
hearts of boy soldiers,
hanging in trees.

Where is the Mirror
That Makes All Things Shine?
The night wind's my Lord.
He cleans the bodies flung in ravines,
and comforts aching women,
standing before their fragile fires.
His breath's a spiral
wide as this galaxy
where nothing is obscured.

Obsidian Butterfly will force you to see
how children sleep in a cardboard box
year after tremulous year. In the span
of their hands, onions, gruel, and
a dangerous abyss
for the people of this sun.
In clouds and mist, their suffering moves.

Something comes to wake you.
Something comes without faltering.
Can you feel it in the twilight?
In your fruits and in your cheeses,
in your signatures?
The gods and goddesses are talking together,
scanning dumpsters and smog,
nuclear playgrounds. They soothe
cholera-stricken geese and the broken
feet of coyotes.

In their diminishing forests
they meet, counting the heartbeats
it will take to make
each face sublime.
Will you acknowledge the love
and faith of our restless earth,
or will you claim the suffering's
too far south while your mouth
samples and measures, calls everything
tangible?

Through darkness, through night
our suffering moves,
a slow quake in the chest, a sigh.
No food and the body will eat itself.
Some of you bluster and do not believe

we have cut the heart of the sky.
You give gasoline to the lords
of your death,
spoon out the sugar,
ignoring its tears.

IN THE SUMMER AFTER
"ISSUE YEAR" WINTER (1873)

I scratch earth around *timpsila*
on this hill, while below me,
hanging in still air, a hawk
searches the creekbed for my brothers.
Squat leaves, I'll braid your roots
into such long ropes, they'll cover
the rump of my stallion.
Withered flower, feed us now
buffalo rot in the waist-high grass.

Hear my sisters laugh?
They dream of feasts, of warriors
to owl dance with them
when this war is over. They don't see
our children eating treebark, cornstalks,
these roots. Their eyes gleam
in shallow cheeks. The wagon people
do not think relationship is wealth.

Sisters, last night the wind
returned my prayer, allowing me to hear
Dog Soldiers singing at Ash Hollow.
I threw away my blanket
stained with lies.
Above the wings of my tipi,
I heard the old woman in *Maka Sica*
sigh for us. Then I knew
the distance of High Back Bone's death-
fire from another world away. Even they
may never stop its motion.

Yesterday at noon, I heard
my Cheyenne sister moan as she waded
through deep snow before soldiers
cut up her corpse to sell
as souvenirs. Are my brothers
here? Ghosts bring all my joy.
I walk this good road between rock
and sky. They dare not threaten with death
one already dead.

THIS GIFT

—for Ernest Whiteman

Within me
wind skims the leaves of sagebrush
under a hot wide sky.
I am more than horse, rider,
hawk, earth and air.
What shapes me, shapes you.
I contain orenda
flaring everywhere you look.
The thick pulse of a spring night.
The quick kiss of a winter daybreak.
Within me
chimeras of smoke leap the ridges
of burning logs.

Within me
the hummingbird's blessing
and the grizzly's wisdom
take root and intertwine
in the cliffs of your spirit.
Such moments when beauty
has seized you, think of me.
I am a persona, the mask
beneath each mask,
the always arriving surf,
the shadow singing toward sunlight,
the stone blossoming in mid-air.
Within me
the full moon climbs the mountains
of your homeland.

HOME BEFORE DARK

—for Ramona Compton

From mountain ridges west,
a reluctant sun alarms clouds to the east,
giving them the salmon tint of dawn,

long before it's due. Other clouds crop
indigo in distant canyons.
Crowheart Butte floats in this last light,

as two Shoshoni women gallop
home before dark. Rain sharpens the wind,
blending the smell of damp earth and sagebrush

with the sound of their sorrel horses.
Sunlight on the brims of their cowboy hats,
these sisters, close to fifty,

ride joyously over this land of a thousand levels.
Beaded roses flashing from their buckles,
they leap wagon ruts, trot over the plateau.

Some folks call them backward, say
they wear shawls in town, herd livestock
for their mother, tan hides and never married.

Clouds group behind them over Black Mountain.
The women head for a southerly range
away from The Lake That Roars

where Shoshoni warriors once hunted
a buffalo bull and his herd.
White as a glacier and twice as mean,

he thundered onto that ice, his herd right behind.
Snow crust enveloping their heavy sighs,
they went down. Since then,

the bull bellows for revenge. Some say
it's only wind through canyons, but others tell
of men who've tasted forbidden meat

and changed to shaggy heads. Clouds stamp out
ledges and ravines, careen closer,
hiding the more difficult terrain.

Now one shadow riding toward the timberline,
the women hurry on. Behind them on Black Mountain,
snow in every crevice, brilliant as a cry.

ONE MORE SIGN

—in memory of Norbert Seabrook Hill

Last night I dreamed you drank coffee
in my kitchen. After telling me of Teapot Dome,
how you roamed by boxcar
through the thirties, you blew four times
in your left fist, nodding at the hiss
of snow outside the screen. One more sign
an island will rise in the Caribbean.

Peering through our earthly dark, you laugh
when I say we won't find you again.
When I explain you cannot be here,
you hitch your belt in back, balancing
that rubber ball above a wound from World War II.
You grip the cup as you once did a drill,
then rise and quickly drink it down.

My uncle, I reach for an embrace,
but brimming through that space, cedar smoke
and the language of rain, lost in its
soliloquy. We didn't listen closely enough
to those rim world people singing in the pines.
We didn't thrill at the wind,
racing through a rhombus of stars.

You knew how secret influences-
leaf, stone, web—converge upon a life
and keep it fed with wonder.
Let others suspect you of false dreams,
an old man speaking to the cosmos
with a pendulum of keys. We whirled
unaware you were the balance wheel.

A week before you left, I thought
you the man crossing Barstow.
On the other side of the street, he
became a stranger, digging in his pocket
for change to buy a paper. Then I feared
your spirit traveled while you catnapped
in a room. Television glow. Closer zoom.

That day you danced away
air around Oneida held such moxie
it lingers on the ridges yet,
incandescent blue. The beating drum.
The beating heart. The galaxy's great arm
sparkled closer with each step
until the heart you often hit
to start again refused. I wait for you
to visit me in dreams. Some moments,
it seems I only need to call
to ask how ball players will arrive
from their court beneath the waves.
Even now, I listen in the dawn
to voices, calm, subterranean.

BEFORE THE WALL

Tonight with the blade's weight
of spackle I obscure
gouges mute chairs made
those nights when smoky windows
choked your dreams
Messages from one accused
live in lightning
ripple toward the freezer

Under long rolls
of thunder I cover them
with ease

Two a.m. orgies of earlier tenants
still show through
His madman's dent
Her cloying repartee
while poisoning their food
the way they left a trail of ashes
nodding like outgoing sails
I've covered them with foothills
with enough snow
to silence
even their relatives

Four a.m. I'm plastering
waves to ride toward your return
In dim light I reach
the first star you saw
in the Sangre de Cristos
I recognize these strains of seaweed

now   Come home   Someone is trying
to lead me astray before
I can claim them

BLACK OUT

—inspired by a painting of the same title by Frank Big Bear

Stumbling down a road at two a.m.,
I'm caught by clouds entering the full moon's ring,
going neon green inside her light.
You do not see me become
a flaming brand, shooting my will
over this dark world. You walk ahead
in the deep shadows of Greenough Park. Memories
of how my family drifts apart
tighten knots of grief and shame
inside my chest.
The only way to cut them loose—
keep a current surging from my will.
Hiya! I shout at the sky
because I intend to hold on until
this sorrow ends even if it never does.

You stop on the bridge, waiting for me
to follow. My feet won't travel right.
The river pounds down from mountains, then hits
those boulders and churns in a dizzy stream.
See them over there?   Ghosts
stretching long lean bodies under those rocks,
then up the banks? My remote control vision
lets me see them rise to shore. Here they come
to walk with us underneath the trees.
I'm gonna hold them hard
against me and tell them all I
could not say to those I've loved.
I try to be real, but never can because,
because each time fear drapes a wet hand
on my shoulder. You know some sweet story

of how we came to be this way?
I want to hug these ghosts so hard
they'll be human, capable of loving
once again.

Hey! You're near me now. Your eyes
hold such bold lights. You're stoned on something
I never got to try. This park's
not that bright, but your madness bubbles
closer than the distance to myself.
I grab you with a hand somebody says is mine.
I can't look straight ahead
to find the car out on the lot,
so I just have to holler once again.
Hiya! Hiya! Seems it
breaks apart this rockwall
in my chest.

See how we can leave in that purple surge
of wind? My belief has all been washed away.
History brought us
to this park after days of toking
and drinking. I feel better without a body.
Now we feel so hollow
even our most eager wants
wait like abandoned doors
under this neon moon.

In the corner of my eye—
my skull's a room
with fifty unknown workmen hammering—
I see those sparrows hopping as they change
to summer leaves. Which one of you threw
this flimsy web across the sky?
You can't fool me!

Where's that crack in history
with its poison seeping through me every day?
My sorrow comes so fast. See the way it flashes
red and slick chartreuse, and it
crushes me so hard, I cannot make a fist
or close my hand.

WAITING FOR ROBINSON

—in memory of Malcolm Lowry, 1909-1957

You nurtured grief until that leap
toward one translucent wave,
wanting a greener world,
a world you couldn't reach,
except in those brief moments
when lights on distant hills
glimmered through the eucalyptus leaves.

Chrome on the back fenders of your coupe
folded into wings. Tar melted
in the cracks near the front tire.
With a tremor in your shoulder,
you let luminol spin you
down Bridge Street in steady traffic.
You passed a vestibule
where under a jardinere, two drunks argued,
who got the tattered blanket, who
the cardboard bed. Robinson,
your gathered up their grief
and stumbled on.

There were no survivors, no shutters
you could close. Dead or insane,
insane or dead. Remembering
how rain told the truth, you tried
to tear the roof away, to stand
under the sun, human and whole,
beyond the fears that seized you.

That July I was eight.
The neighbor lady hid behind venetian

blinds. Warm evenings, I'd wait
until an eye peered from the even shade.
Across a table made of dust,
you taunt me now. Aloof chimera,
how I wanted you to find a green world
spinning in other earth-dark eyes.

One hand waves from a train.
Another from outgoing tide.
Gulls cry, search for the hand no one
could reach, as it held a card
complete with birth star, braided rug,
blue crystal and an easy chair.

Don't believe these melancholy lines.
The summer I turned twenty-eight,
I heard you hitched to Salton Sea,
away from rain and eucalyptus.
The glow from your cigarette
danced at dusk in the desert air.
You found it serene, dry there, though
not as green as you once hoped.

From The Sun Itself

While something hummed along the river,
I sat on a wooded hill in Spring,
playing my flute to fluttering green.
At my feet, a bellwort and a fern.

A white pine churned above me.
From the sun itself, the bellwort's flame.
An oak branch snapped, then crashed behind me,
as he came through the canopy.

A huge hawk folded, fell, then opening
his mantle, swooped under oaks with no qualm.
With the mastery of ashes, he twisted, lifted
and turned, breezing easily on broad wings.

I clung to a high note, more for my health
than his. No stranger to the scheming wind,
he hit the rim of the hill, flicked
his red tail and broke into blue.

The mottled light underneath his wings
scattered into beeches below.
Heady with flight, I stood silent, for
he knew what the human heart renounces.

He circled east and flew to the sun itself.
So drawn to him by my longing,
I didn't hear the deepening drone.
As bellwort, fern and pine bough grew greener,

the chopper's keen blade lagged for a moment,
after a dawn raid on the gypsy moths.
The pilot may never know he was swinging
the fierce edge of our twilight.

Breaking Trail

Here basswood leaves soak up
evening sun, their phosphorescent leaves
glistening like scum on the surface
of the pond we passed just now.

Our children are leaving, taking
the rue and the red light of sunrise
with them. Soon the wind will pile
their clothes in the southwest corner

of the sky. We followed trails our parents
took and others. We cut our own brush
oftentime. We pushed through mud so deep,
our children knew its danger and detoured.

Yet on days like this in midsummer,
singing fills my soul when
under the ecstacy of leaves
we find the way worms work leaves

into lace and wing. Stepping over a log,
you hold out your hand behind you.
I grasp your warm fingers
and once again we trudge in sunlight

as it falls along these ridges.
I'm grateful basswood leaves, wide
and heart-shaped, never wave goodbye,
even in high wind.

Sometimes I dawdle as the trail turns,
remembering those I've lost, places level
with promise, but the killdeer cries
from a distant hill and I move on.

FOGBOUND

Last night
the moon let her uncarded wool
spill over these houses
and hills

Now
beyond my door
the woods recede into a labyrinth
of latent waves
while the pomp pomp of dew
dripping from eaves
measures the music
of her passage

From his fencepost
a storm-colored rooster
cocks his head
listening
for the distant tread of the sun

but the moon fashioned even stones
into sponges
When it doesn't come
he crows

All the unnamed beings
beyond this crossroad
answer
who are you that the sun
should come first
to your flat eyes

Above this maze of edges
flies a woodpecker
whose red head sways like a lantern
in the sea's spindrift

I lift my life
to the moon this autumn morning
toast with my breath
all she's left me
I dance down the road in her honor
dance back   singing
rapt in the wet wool
of her buried world

where nothing is discerned
or decided very long
where bushes and branches multiply
into meandering herds
into egrets rising in frothy silence

where every flicker
of lifting mist
bears witness to another encounter

Through such a world
I'd walk to Guatemala
carrying the moon's cochineal
still living in my cape
I'd wear them
draped like crimson kisses
through those turbulent mountains

if only
I knew by now
you had crossed the river

where thick fibers have scrubbed off
summer's green

There oaks gleam as copper and umber
as wood voles slumbering
underneath

if only

that spider hadn't captured
the world's four winds
in the roof's overhang
In her spangled web
they strain
while she works the whorl and spindle
of herself
In her web the polar lights
the muddy fragrance of March lilies
the secret echoes
of swallows perched in hedgerows
after a summer rain

while you head west
my alien
into a subdued morning

AGAINST ANNIHILATION

— for Jacob A. Hill

When I found eraser dust
from "You must do your math"
left on my desk this morning, I thought of how
I love to see your face,
at once so familiar, so foreign.
Soon, you will be a man
in a country born from war,
in a country that renews its pride
by making cluster-bombs. But this morning
we are safe on our street and I can watch
your spirit shimmer around you
when you laugh.

At this moment, the joy of antelope twins
who bounded before you on the day
of your birth overtakes you.
You grow bold, curious
to the point of danger,
tramping through jack pines,
setting up camps. Your nomadic soul
follows the wind's way—
whatever arrives, arrives.
Yet you never stay out too long

before the coolness of the turtle clan
glides over your shoulders.
Then your turtle heart hedges
and you hoard string,
bits of tin, railroad ties,
like gatherers who abided
under ancient maples.

You grow so hard on yourself, hibernating,
building robots in your room,
your blood blooming under dreaming seas,
inaccessible to me,
though at times like these
you stand before an open window
like my father.

At such moments, do you ponder
just what phenolphthalein means?
This poem asks the earth
to offer you her care,
to remind you that your grandfathers
lived here for five hundred thousand years.
They followed The Loon,
so it may also guide
your running through the humming night.

At distances greater than your twelve years,
through the silhouettes
of starker fears, may these blessings
find you still
wonderously alive
in this world that prizes
annihilation.

SPEAKING THROUGH THE GENERATIONS

When the last red-tail hawk flies south
with the weight of cold rain on his wings,
we'll remember your strength, grandfathers.

When the moon's horn tilts and a wall of cloud
brings fevers and pain, we'll soothe each brow
and remember your faith, grandmothers.

When ravens tuck underwing
the loneliness of six thousand journeys,
we'll remember your courage, grandfathers.

When frost clouds the bean vine and corn,
and starvation wakes us with its cranky burden,
we'll remember your generosity, grandmothers.

Although we've been scattered, we keep alive
the memory of your voices, speaking
through the generations.

On this earth, our Turtle Island, we know our needs
dovetail the needs of those to come
and the needs of those who've gone.

Huddled in this dusk, in these intricately turning times,
we contemplate your visions and your warnings.
What need have we to appraise the stars?

UNBINDING ANGER

In this city of verdigris domes,
in this house where lonely winds
sabotage remembering,
anger knotted my insides

with skeins of glistening thread.
When the doctor cuts it all away,
pain will change perception
in ways that will could never do.

In these moments I think of gifts
I gave you, gifts I didn't defend
when you condemned them over and over
and over again. It took time

to understand your fear sprang
from our common wounds, the legacy
of surviving this era
of oppression, the ways we had

to live when the country cut
our grandfathers' hair and stole
the eyes of our elders to keep
in damp museums. With boots

on our voice boxes, they ripped apart
clans as they did the Great Wood.
In a story, in a well, in another wind,
you might have loved my child

the one who pays attention
to the ripe smell of worms dying
on sidewalks after hard dark rain.
We might have healed by gathering flecks

of flotsam floating over the dam
on this broken river.
Somewhere a girl prizes an aimless path,
running barefoot on the grass

of crisp blue mornings. Somewhere a boy
carries a leafy branch
above him down the road, waving
its elation. I want them back.

They will not come alone,
but bring the old woman I'll become,
the one driven to dance lifelong
with the bones of wishes.

Unbinding this anger has renewed
my belief that love's rapture doesn't rest
in oblivion, but leaps beyond
language toward greater mysteries.

Our children search their marrow
for strange paths into tomorrow.
They dare to find that place
where the voices that judged

our worth before we lived it
recede into the mists
of our colonized histories.
One image sustains me

as they journey on—a love
strong as palm leaves
rising in sunlight. Naturally, one end grows
frayed and points its fingers,

but the leaf itself grows broad,
loosens wide pleats like a generous skirt.
When I feel alone, it twirls
the earth's boundless green energy above me.

REPARATIONS

I drove from Mazopa
through hills that aged with every turn
where trees grew
denser than liquid dark.
I went up and over crests
down around ravines
without seeing another car.

When fog enveloped every view,
I peered into the windshield as I slowed,
knowing in these hills
Traverse de Sioux was signed,
feeling that those who long ago
loved these green coulees
would have camped in this cloudland
to dream of deer.

Lost in my machinery,
I pushed on, even though in the glowing clouds
I lost all direction—hills swallowed me whole.
I drove over the tops of trees.
Risks like these kept me shaking.
You were alone on that same road
and if I had stopped,
we might have met
under the green drifts of that canopy.

So much of my life was like that road,
where I longed to stop,
but didn't dare,
urging myself to push on somewhere

unimportant,
unaware how close a friend
was passing by.

Reaching the clear air of the river after midnight,
I gunned the car around a curve.
Where only dark had been,
there from the reeds, a herd of twenty deer
bounded around the fenders.
The doe worked hard
to shift the young buck's elegant hurdling
away from my hard lights.

Red eyes and budding horns.
His hind hooves hit my right front fender.
I too have a son, passing
through this world's happenstance.
When I stopped and searched for those deer
whose ancient energy invests
the summer wood, all of them were gone.
I asked forgiveness,
but my voice plied the reeds
like a finger of wind.

II

All the long way home deer came out to graze
and graze me with their eyes.
I have maimed more than deer
with my impatience, with my driving full tilt
on a curve where I could slow
and meld the motion of the night with my soul.
These words
are reparations for that deer.
I leave them in this bundle filled

with rose and purple winter twilights
and the feathered dark of trees
in hard packed snow.
This bundle contains a healing sound—
a blast of wind to waken trees.

Later you said you too
had hit an animal on that road.
We speak of it six years later,
a quiet circumstance
unlike marriage or children leaving home,
but subtle all the same in how it helps us age.
Wisdom lives in places
where we are forced to stop
with wind in our wet eyes.

They Mention A Word Like 'Welcome'

Early morning shadows arrive
in the southwest corner of the porch.
They jangle the lilies of the valley,
creating a lithe breeze. Perched
on a wire, the sparrow hardly feels
its shadow, low in the gravel,
lift a wing feather for flight.

In a squinting noon,
shadows nestle in thickets,
spangle the deep limbs of elms,
hover in crickets' crazy eyes.
Only curs call to those shadows
of the sun which rove every
eleven years over the full moon.

Shadows watch what no one else does,
then wade into our lives.
The friendly ones
stretch rocks under a sloshing wave,
or spin a dizzy pattern
in the school yard's din.
One shadow alone
can lengthen the haze on a river,
or hold a heavy peony
prisoner to its stem.

Our shadows arrive before we do.
If we could touch them, they'd flutter
like moths caught in a fist.
As we die, they mention

a word like 'welcome',
leading us into oak groves
where the hopeful ones
gather our aging sins.

Only then do they ease us up
until we glide without them
inside the essential world
like dandelion seed,
blown across midsummer meadows.

TWO

The Peacemaker spoke to the tyrant, Tha-do-dah-ho, "These Lords who now stand all around you have now accepted the good tidings of Peace and Power, which signifies that now hereafter the shedding of human blood shall cease, for our Creator, the Great Spirit, never intended that man should engage in any such work of destruction of human life. There are many who have perished in the direction you are now facing, and these Lords have come to induce you to join them, so that the shedding of human blood might cease, and the good tidings of Peace and Power might prevail."

— from "Traditional History of the Confederacy of the Six Nations," related at Ohsweken Council House, August 17, 1900, recorded in *The Transactions of the Royal Society of Canada*, 1911.

PHILADELPHIA FLOWERS

I

In the cubbyhole entrance to Cornell and Son,
a woman in a turquoise sweater
curls up to sleep. Her right arm seeks
a cold spot in the stone to release its worry
and her legs stretch
against the middle hinge.

I want to ask her in for coffee,
to tell her go sleep in the extra bed upstairs,
but I'm a guest,
unaccustomed to this place
where homeless people drift along the square
bordering Benjamin Franklin Parkway.

From her portrait on the mantel,
Lucretia Mott asks when
will Americans see
how all forms of oppression blight
the possibilities of a people.
The passion for preserving Independence Square

should reach this nameless woman, settling
in the heavy heat of August,
exposed to the glare of every passerby.
What makes property so private? A fence?
No trespassing signs? Militia ready to die for it
and taxes? Lights in the middle storeys

of office buildings blaze all night above me.
Newspapers don't explain how wealth
is bound to these broken people.

North of here, things get really rough.
Longshoremen out of work bet on eddies
in the Schuylkill River.

Factories collapse to weed
and ruptured dream. Years ago, Longhouse sachems
rode canoes to Philadelphia,
entering these red brick halls.
They explained how
the law that kept them unified

required a way to share the wealth.
Inside the hearths of these same halls,
such knowledge was obscured,
and plans were laid to push all Indians
west. This city born of brotherly love
still turns around this conflict.

Deeper in the dusk,
William Penn must weep
from his perch on top of City Hall.
Our leaders left this woman in the lurch.
How can there be democracy
without the means to live?

II

Every fifteen minutes
a patrol car cruises by. I jolt awake
at four a.m. to sirens screeching
and choppers lugging to the hospital heliport
someone who wants to breathe.

The sultry heat leads me
to the window. What matters? This small
square of night sky and two trees
bound by a wide brick wall.
All around, skyscrapers

are telling their stories
under dwindling stars. The girders
remember where Mohawk ironworkers stayed
that day they sat after work
on a balcony, drinking beer.

Below them, a film crew caught
some commercials. In another room above
a mattress caught fire and someone flung it
down into the frame. A woman in blue
sashayed up the street

while a flaming mattress,
falling at the same speed as a flower,
bloomed over her left shoulder.
Every fifteen minutes
a patrol car cruises by. The men inside

mean business. They understood the scene.
A mattress burning in the street
and business deadlocked. Mohawks
drinking beer above it all.
They radioed insurrection,

drew their guns, then three-stepped
up the stairs. Film crews caught the scene,
but it never played. The Mohawks
didn't guess a swat team had moved in.
When policemen blasted off their door,

the terrified men shoved a table
against the splintered frame.
They fought it out.
One whose name meant Deer got shot
again and again. They let him lie

before they dragged him by his heels
down four flights of stairs. At every step,
he hurdled above his pain
until one final leap
gained him the stars.

The news reported one cop broke his leg.
The film's been banished to a vault. There are
no plaques. But girders whisper at night
in Philadelphia. They know the boarding house,
but will not say. They know as well what lasts
        and what falls down.

III

Passing Doric colonnades of banks
and walls of dark glass,
passing press-the-button-visitors-please
Liberty Townhouses, I turned
up Broad Street near the Hershey Hotel
and headed toward the doorman
outside the Bellevue. Palms and chandeliers inside.
A woman in mauve silk and pearls stepped into the street.

I was tracking my Mohawk grandmother
through time. She left a trace

of her belief somewhere near Locust and Thirteenth.
I didn't see you, tall, dark, intense,

with three bouquets of flowers in your hand.
On Walnut and Broad, between the Union League
and the Indian Campsite, you stopped me,
shoving flowers toward my arm.

"At least, I'm not begging," you cried.
The desperation in your voice
spiraled through my feet while I fumbled the few bucks
you asked for. I wanted those flowers—

iris, ageratum, goldenrod and lilies—
because in desperation
you thought of beauty. I recognized
the truth and human love you acted on,

your despair echoing my own.
Forgive me. I should have bought more
of those Philadelphia flowers, passed hand
to hand so quickly, I was stunned a block away.

You had to keep your pride, as I have done,
selling these bouquets of poems
to anyone who'll take them. After our exchange,
grandmother's tracks grew clearer.

I returned for days, but you were never there.
If you see her — small, dark, intense,
with a bun of black hair and the gaze of an orphan,
leave a petal in my path.
Then I'll know I can go on.

IV

Some days you get angry enough
to question. There's a plan out east
with a multitude of charts and diagrams.

They planned to take the timber, the good soil.
Even now, they demolish mountains.
Next they'll want the water and the air.

I tell you they're planning to leave our reservations
bare of life. They plan to dump their toxic
wastes on our grandchildren. No one wants to say

how hard they've worked a hundred years.
What of you, learning how this continent's
getting angry? Do you consider what's in store for you?

BEING INDIAN

Being Indian
she felt sand bags weigh her heart,
looking out the window
at the maze of lights and man-made squares,
row on row of houses,
one never hers, traffic humming
past office buildings
where the suits took her solitude
and forced it to become
this suffocation.

Her daughter walked out there, eyes
blazing with manufactured
madness, open to every bum
or bungler who might want to smack
a teen-age girl or send her to some clammy hell
in heartbreak.
Her daughter was so willful
as she destroyed each brain cell.
The t.v. flashed its tyranny
as it told her she
could never be recognized
as real.

Her son stuck to the shadows,
beaming everything with the flashlight
of his rage. She was afraid he never saw
sunlight and that when he finally found
the river of his manhood,
the military would come
for their blood offering and find his rage

of suitable temperature and his batteries
suitably weak, so he could learn to kill
other brown beings like himself.

His rage, her rage,
healthy in this time and place
where Indians live.

Being Indian
she felt it good to dream.
She imagined a house inside the hills
on her reservation.
Those hills like humpback whales could rise
in the sea-green mists of morning.
Perhaps her children could return
to the earth that nourished them.
Cities that sucked them off the land
could surely blow them back again.
When that time came,
her grandchildren would learn how good
it feels to nurture seeds
and touch warm earth,
as their people did
for five hundred thousand years,
how good it feels
to praise human worth inside this hoop
of living forms. They will learn
how much courage they will need
to understand the story
of their poverty.

Being Indian
she had faith enough to let her burdens
fall. She taught her children

how to tease, how to believe
in the invisibles, to know wisdom
and trickery often appear in the same
ravishing disguise.

Being Indian
she lit a smudge and waited
for the dawn, quieting her thoughts, her fears,
peering through the buildings
for the sun.

THE PATRIARCH'S POWER

I

Although I held your hand
when we walked through fields where stars bright
as lances led us on,
I never noticed your hesitant step,

the knife in your boot, young man,
or the way you chose roads steeped in shadow.
Every time we turned,
I used that old compass as a guide,

never guessing what my mother
called an heirloom had busted in Boston long ago.
Itching for Indian land,
the salesman jammed the magnets.

While I thought we were heading
north, the proper path, we aimed into the unknown
hardship of the south. I had
grand illusions, dreaming we were aspens rippling

heart-shaped leaves into the wind
of a mountainside. We'd age into an amber tide
present in the present
of each day. I didn't understand your recurring dream

of the red, seven-headed
dragon who keeps rising from the sea.
I forgot the power
of water panthers whose waves of chaos

wedge their capricious coils
into our destinies. So I brought you, child,
into these cities,
glittering with lights, detached from night's expanse.

II

Here our breath grew restless
and we never stopped to watch rain cool the horizon.
All the wealth of summer
faded on your arms as the wild child you once were,

brave enough to face
the wooded night alone, grew into a man-child
haunted by hidden wounds.
We slid through rooms like snails in their starched houses,

never glimpsing how
our silver trails entwined. We ate denial,
addicted to its gummy taste,
creating catastrophes to keep our sense

of isolation keen,
while the real horrors we could not permit ourselves
to name came with us.
You drew men flayed with knives in their necks,

ripped apart by secrets
worming through their wasting hearts. Piercing together
the worries you share
now and again from a corner of hurt, I imagine

a patriarch's cruel embrace
shaped this distrust of your own human beauty.

You cannot tell anyone
for fear of collapsing into rage and hard revenge.

III

The patriarch's power
has left hard scars for generations. To live with love
we've balanced them in the arbors
of our souls. With the echo of one word,

an avalanche begins, offering
in its roiling wake a new face for the mountain.
With time, we can allow ourselves
to name brutality. Then water panthers turn

their churning power toward our confidence.
They too believe love's our truest legacy.
Love will heal our pain and guide our worth
aiding earth's renewal. She lets her scars

become her as she goes.
When a fire proves too fierce, she answers with a sea.
This great mystery
strengthens us when we perceive in fleeting ways

we never dwell alone.
Every feeling changes all that moves.
I comfort but cannot
make the meaning of those repeating shadows

become more clear. You may find
in the scent of sage that courage to behold the sun
setting in unsettling times
and in the warmth of the evening star,

your innocence again.

OUR DIFFERENT STORY

After my father returned from the war
he gave each of us a mask to wear
like the one his mother
gave him, made of gauze.

Wear this he said so they won't see
that you belong to a different story.
When you enter their world
what they do
won't hurt so much.

We wore the flimsy gauze that smelled
like a dusty curtain. It tickled our ears,
ruffled over our arms and draped down our backs
like a bride's long veil.
Its moire patterns dazzled our sleep
but we still
lifted it from our faces
to dance inside our different story.

When we got hurt or grew afraid,
we chided each other. You don't
wear it right. We never thought its whisper
could run around our heads for years.
Do you hear it muttering now, my sisters?

We hugged each other
when it grew too tight against our eyes
like a sour bandage.
We squinted past its mottled light
at dark green fields beyond its threshold.

Boyfriends who refused to wear it
had it stapled on their faces
in places called prison and boarding school.
Inez told father the gauze was cutting us
whenever we tried to rip it
from our foreheads.

But father's mask by then
became the cast of light in winter.
He couldn't remember the day
his mother gave him his. He felt our pain,
but could not stop
what had become its steady hum.
Do you hear it now, my sisters?
That television in a far-off room?

I find it fluttering over me at times
like those nights my sister
threw a sheet high as the blue stucco ceiling.
Its cool nap
skipped down my face
my thighs. If I could
lie still enough, I'd hear the sound of dying.
When I walked highways in despair,
I heard the leaves applauding
where its edges frayed and my first face
was undisguised.

My children find gauze everywhere
they go. One in their games
had mica woven in the warp. Its transparent lace
constrains each heart. They say
it's just a sparkler
they can light and watch be spent.
I cannot stop
its pattern from traveling up their arms.

I tell you sisters, I'm afraid
they will grow used
to the same cuts,
more fond of their own wounds
than lust or love.

Father cannot help us now. In our time,
we have to struggle from these wrappings,
cocoons in need of cracking,
tougher on breasts than corsets,
hotter at times than a cast,
filled with a multitude of insufferable itches.

I danced around the dumpster
until mine ripped
and the story bloomed above me in the dark.
Only then could I recognize the moon.
I plan to pry apart
the glint inside each wave
and ask the sun to melt
the remnants of this haze
around me. Then, I hope the earth
will stun me with her power
and I'll gaze at each of you
free of its distortions.

Remember, my sisters,
the sea and sky, the mountains and hollows
wait for us to break loose
and follow that music we hear,
music that urges us to move
into the mysteries of our America.
Come join me.

OF LIGHT, WATER AND GATHERED DUST

Above Chequamegon Bay
two immense assemblies of summer clouds
collide, flare with messages,
and rumble their rejection.
With massive strides, they
edge each other. Bunch-backed by a load
of cauliflower, the eastern front
drives daggers of rain
into the dove-grey water
between them.

The western flyers snap green whips,
forcing cruise ships home.
When the lightning flashes,
you name a shore hovering
in mid-air. Other islands out there
are shrewd as submerging monsters,
eyes flickering in the dusk.

The gulls' transparent cries
are blown along a low cliff.
Wings awry from wind,
they read it, then balance again,
swinging like pendents beyond us.
Crickets resist the wind and sing.

Orange and red lightning
explodes in dizzy loops. Two flashes
zig from top down cloud.
The bay surges over rocks,
its fish aware of an upper world.

"Look!" I say. "In that flash, the oak grove
we walked through last spring."
Crickets approve, sing louder than before.
As shreds of cauliflower fall earthward,
houselights on Madeleine Island dim.

Above the scattering clouds,
Jupiter, close as the motel door,
and the Milky Way, no longer remote,
but bright as your laughter in the dark.
The footprints of souls who walked
this earth plane whirl toward us,
through us, beyond us, into us.

Born of light, water
and gathered dust, we grope
for one another's hand,
and trust the galaxy's embrace,
as leaves trust air, as thunder, its cloud.

You fling your cigarette over the rail.
It grows a tail and travels
through a slow, glowing arc.
For that moment,
even crickets pause.

LETTING GO

Under Blue Dome
where mountain spirits wander,
he curls in a green bedroll,
listening, listening
thirteen years old.

When the tent flap flutters,
he remembers T. J. stuffing gorp
into his backpack,
the grizzly snorting all night
through their camp in Sequoia,
until the dawn ranger reported:
Bear disturbance. No one injured.

In a wind-swollen flash
of sparks and ash, I hope he hears
a mountain spirit dancing nearby,
her stony breath pressing him
as much as the womanly night.

I had to let him go,
my gangly eagle child, struggling
to ride currents of life's uplifting wind,
yet then, as now and always,
when pines mimic ocean swells,
I want his radiant childhood
to carry him back to me,
like phosphorus returning
to a warm southern sea.

Even though
night's rapture grows between us,
each time he telephones,
distant as my own myth of mountains,
I listen for
the shift in tone
that tells me he's encountered
his true mother.

At daybreak
her iridescent song
drifts from a canyon
hidden in our dreams,
and we seem to rise from our own power,
so skilled is her vision.

I had to let him go
encounter his true father
in rings of evenstar shine and boulders.
Perched on a limb
of a salt-rimmed tree,
watching the heavy sea brighten
as twilight grows,
I hope he'll learn manhood needs
both action and repose.

How I long to save him
from the miseries of war.
Enough have died so far
in this quest for empire.

His true parents strengthen
his willingness to love,
his high-strung mirth
in the boardwalk's glare,

his dragging T. J.
from the undertow.

Cicadas flutter their flimsy
but persistent wings, until the buzzsaw
of their passion stings the July heat.

As storm clouds rise
and rain pommels oaks,
I notice in a lightning flash
the road's grown thin.
Suffering this sea change,
I peek again from the kitchen window.
Every light is on,
every curtain, open.

VAN GOGH IN THE OLIVE GROVE

"We do not know what will happen to us tomorrow, but whatever it may be, think of me, think of me." —Vincent Van Gogh

You walked into the olive grove
outside St. Remy
and knew you lied about everything
but this—only someone brave
could stand among these trees
that know how deep the wounds we give
ourselves. Once again the sun
struck root into your bones.
Once again you felt flung against this earth
and reeling still.

Reeling from an illness that overtook
your will, you drew a cipher in the shadow
and listened to the ancient conversation
of olive leaves and wind.
Is that why you painted them
bunched around themselves,
nodding like normal men
around a dining table?

Each one who walks alone
feels the same trick of sunlight.
In that suspended moment before dark,
shadows winnow amethyst wings
through the burnished grasses.

Did you sense a spark, a warning
from within, before you cracked apart
like glass flung in a furnace? On your sleeve,
a cicada clings, brown chip of earth
against the sunlight's sting.

You grieved for the decline and decadence
of things. "Adieu!" the great sun cries,
stroking your stubbled face,
changing hue each degree it fell.
Energies in your arm exalted that whirlpool,
broke through certain barriers, gaits and walls
to graft an apparition to our world.

I found the hidden path you painted in the grove.
Mountains waver on the rim like a mirage.
Sometimes in the woods, the sun grabs hold
of me. Then I hear light sizzling in the leaves
and feel ciphers wedged inside each stone.

Then every bit of dirt or stem glistens
as I do inside the sun. When this feeling comes,
I think of you in the olive grove,
taking in the wealth of those few trees,
the mountain farther than anyone believes.
I've lied about everything, but this.

WOLF SMOKE

I'm that nomad woman tossed from the lap of dawn,
faithful only to the yellow dust
driving itself to the sea.

Look at me, guard of a riddle, this Great Wall
where a wedge of five horsemen rides
on watch for us. Barbarians, you say.

Feel motion a magnet in your blood
when you signal from the tower,
lighting your fire of wolf dung.

Even while wolf smoke skitters across
the turquoise dome of our common home, the sky,
I'll still ricochet over my astonishing wasteland.

My orphan blood bears witness
to the crime of being kept out,
my crime of blasting through,

the crime for us to speak together of our love
for wind, humming as it does,
from the Gobi to the Sahara,

from the Atacama to the Great Plains.
On my tongue, it never tastes the same.
Yet that same wind

now ruffles our hair. On each strand it writes
the names of those we've loved,
the names of those we've lost.

Why must you prod those masons
hemmed inside ten feet of stone?
My longing to know you lights the wolf's red eyes

when it meets your fire this coming twilight.
Out here, cold rain means ravine,
but the sheen on mulberry leaves

often draws us into dancing.
Dark as roots, your eyes uncover mine and make
me hesitate, waiting for some splendor

to rise within this moment
where we yet may call a greeting
instead of bleeding for each other.

EMPRESS HSAIO-JUI SPEAKS HER MIND

These last ten years
I didn't see our love dance in candlelight.
All this time we've been walking
down the dark halls
toward our tomb. Every gesture
born of love lights ten thousand candles.
In that light, Wanli,
Emperor of the Middle Kingdom,
the keystone of the arch
is poised above your head.

When you glanced at me
that moment, I found more riches
than the Phoenix cap of woven gold
or the jade cup whose handles
claw my heart.
First Empress Hsaio-Ching married your jade
and marble and I, the minor wife,
a green sea-mist hovering in your hazel eyes.
When no one else walks near,
you take my hand and lead me
underground. Sometimes we crawl
along the passages of this tomb, burdened
by afterimages of artisans dying
where they dreamed your greater glory.

Drunk inside silk curtains,
you trace our childhoods
with your finger on my belly.
Could you deny the cosmos
which declared you emperor at ten
and me your concubine?

In our next lives, let's be wrens
chirping in the cedars near this tomb,
flitting over the raked sand
in light like that under our lagoon.
Two wrens flying from Tiger
to Dragon Mountain.
Common spring birds
only a foreigner would notice.

No, you say. Impossible.
For childhood's lightest step
and greatest dread accompanies
each gesture even after we are dead
and these mahogany coffins hold us.
You saw dragons soaring
above the blue roof tiles of your temple
last month when you offered the first grain.
You're certain that great wheel of stars
above anticipates your claim
to create this beauty
at the cost of thirty thousand lives.

Wanli, you win
for you are emperor. Besides, you make me
delight in the glow
of a thousand times ten thousand
flames calmly consuming the wick
of our lives. You also want the two of us
to fly. A dragon and two phoenixes
whirl toward the summer sun,
while courtisans left below
smell the perfume we leave, rising.
Lights left from our love
will tremble in the draft.

Which of our longings
will the great wheel grant us?
Wanli, you laugh
tempting my elbow
with your yellow sleeve
again.

TRAVELING

The moon on the rim of my world
skims westward over ripples of cirrus haze.
It is the orange sail of a junk
I follow, traveling in indigo twilight.

Do you know in order to sleep
I read Tibetan Poetry? Chinese History?
The xun wavers in unfamiliar air
quicksilver above the gearing down

of trucks leaving the nearby freeway.
Sometimes when I lift the lid of my cup,
tea leaves catch my heart in hidden currents
and I remember orchid petals

trembling in the Tea House of Du Fu
in his City of Brocade.
He knew what strengths arrive
with exile. Sometimes those lagoons

inundate my daily life
and I wait while ripples of jade
surge against my shoulders.
I wait while the mountains of Leshan

unravel roads around the horizon
of my afternoon. We travel
with common heartbeats now
though half a world away,

you, too, write toward dawn alone.
Does someone watch you from beyond
for that single indiscretion?
Tiptoeing across tightropes of ideology,

carrying only the asylum
of my words, I want to reach you,
but I cannot make them minarets
or gorges, breath crystals drifting

in an azure sky, the way
your native tongue looks to me on paper.
You said a gold thread binds all things
together. Can I find it here?

Sometimes I long for sweet-sour carp
and garlic shoots. Do you ever scour
the undergound for books
on Indian nations beyond your eastern sea?

True to the drum and bell sound of my soul,
I dance these pictures into wind
and send them over the backs of ocean waves,
because I wanted you to know

every now and then I cannot sleep
until I touch my fingers to the earth
to feel if you're still rising
on the other side.

Storm Warning

On torrid summer nights,
when weathermen warn of whirlwinds,
of severe storms,
newly born, southwest of your streetlight,
welcome the rain and dance. Run out
in the cold spray, open your arms
so rain will run over your palms,

into your armpits. Welcome the rain
and dance. Leap over lawns
in your pajamas, lean into crescendos
of wind, eyelids fluttering,
hair unraveling with every lunge.
Let neighbors cower in the southwest corner,
pondering their insurance.

Your assurance rides with rain,
so stomp through puddles, spin in rhythm
with thunders. Lightning will loosen
that hard ache in your shoulders, the grasses
growing spongy under your feet, your spry step
veering over the vestibules
of earthworms.

Welcome the rain and dance. Feel summer
surge through your thighs as thunder booms
with longing for his full length of sky.
If wind wants your house,
let him have it. Look up as you whirl
through the storm. Feel these warm blessings
falling straight down.

PREGUNTAS

—for Professor Hernan Vidal

In the classroom at Folwell Hall
while the afternoon sun warmed the oak panels around us,
you said, "Your bones contain your people's history."
I had to write it down.
In my home state,
in Medford, Wisconsin, there is a bounty
for brown women like me.

The sign at the local pizzeria
announces "The First Annual Indian Shoot".
I felt the bones in my fingers
and I scruffed them across the sign.
"It is not the first," the right fingerbones sang.
"It has never been annual," the left ones added.

To some in this classroom, I may look
like a deer
or a quail preening in the back corner of the room
against the wall and window.
I warble in the air of the classroom,
Ok, Ok, I'll be that bird,
la guarda barranca who lives in these ravines
on the underside of American history.

From these thickets,
in the shadow of his years,
my father sits at our table
near the window telling stories.
The west wind knew how to listen
and sometimes sends his voice back to me
whenever my blood falters.

I welcomed his singing
in the dark, his sobbing
in the dark, paralyzed at times
in his struggle against the daily snare
of being declared worthless.

Because of him, I know
my flesh is corn come from earth.
Because of him, I know
my body is a hologram
of all that is and ever was.
What fear drives them?
What makes them want to annihilate
these memories in our bones and blood?

Bones breaking silence, speak.
Words finding wings, fly.
Wings bringing clouds, whirl.
Clouds bearing rain, fall
on those fields that uphold justice.

You taught me to consider the greater scene
where the process plays into deaths
we can't deny. They want hurt and rage
to cement our bones, so we can't dance by them.
They want us drunk and armed
whenever we ride across northern Wisconsin.
They'll call us terrorists and savages,
call newsmen to see
our hides tacked to garage doors
because we question the word "civilized"
openly against this treeless horizon,
because we declare ourselves
original human beings.

Sometimes across your face
floats a cloud of loneliness and loss,
of solidarity with those who suffer.
You draw schema on the blackboard
to reveal the wheel of fragments
in which we live. Although you clearly
show us contradictions like gears,
grinding every one of us into sand,
the schema have not taught me as much
as the sundown cloud across your face
when you speak of justice.

You have helped me understand
their fear of the dark
is not my identity.
Their Indian Shoot doesn't create
more wiggle room for a few more fish.
It's not about fish, but fake blue lakes.
Not about trees, but copper.

Sometimes the wind brings to my window
my father's voice with the voices of others.
Akwesasne, Tlaltelolco, Lac du Flambeau,
El Salvador. Because of you, I trust
bones breaking silence will speak,
words finding wings will fly,
wings bringing clouds will whirl,
and whirling clouds,
filled with oblique rain,
will fall on those fields
that answer these questions
of justice.

You Call Me Less Than All I Am

For ages and ages
under clear summer nights
I bridged wind and stars.

See how I live?
Every bit of bark, every limb and flat leaf
      explores a different span.
My canopy of edges
      nourished the origins
      of your blood, your brooding.

Call me a cedar growing from rocks.
Call me the record of earth's blessing.
Watch me curve, coil, throw a sinewy hook,
then come murmur with me.
Let go the rigid patterns
      of streets and submarines.

My resin scents the earth
as I grope through the velvet warmth
of dirt, just beyond your reach
just in need of your touch.
My creators remind me of my girth—
my leaves stop stars before your eyes.

When the wind fills me
      the music I am
clings to every branch.
Through me, see the processions of stars,
the spiral dance of earth,
through me, feel your backbone
and your worth.

What shelter, without my green youth?
My spirit always faces south,
      and yours?
Even when I creak, I offer my home
      to katies that did,
      to katies that didn't,
      and you?

Wish from an Office Window

—for Marti Mahalyi

How I long to be a bird of prey,
    hawk spiraling over plains, wingtips whistling under currents
        of blue summer domes whose faces are forever
            bulging, changing, indulging every whim
                of current until I snap down, and
                    pull the fear-frozen rabbit
                      with me into sky.

How I long to be a bug,
    dragonfly dancing above that crest of sun reflected
        in each wave, feeling dews douse me, my tacky feet
            stuck to buckbean, until my wierd belly
                finds its narrow hunger and I split, hang, flit
                  anonymous in air above
                    nurseries of mosquitoes.

How I long to be a meteor,
    whizzing down alleys of glowing worlds,
        not yet named, known, waited for, counted on,
            consuming myself in one farewell flash,
                pulled by fences of forces, dark drains
                  of stars, dwarves daring me
                    carry more wind, while giants watch
                      me spin and glitter by every
                        stoplight nebula.

How I long to be a sky,
    thrilled by sweet pangs of lightning, buoying ten thousand winds
    tirelessly, the whole delicious earth spinning in my arms,
        my waist engulfed with circlet of stars, my heart
            wheeling in holy blue, my veils flying toward
                a warm galaxy, both mirror and reaper to
                  smaller horizons.

THE EARTH AND I ARE ONE

I

Out of the layers of stars,
one star whose fragrance fills the wind
      comes dancing.
Out of the layers of air,
the sun, our brother, flies.
We are wrapped in his wings.
His golden glance hurls us spiraling
though space
      through time
           through dark.

In dawn light we walk gratefully
      in a living world.
The living wind breathes us,
moves in and out,
      spins in and out, up and
through spaces in the blue,
spaces where the fading stars twinkle back.

Shadows lengthen and grow bold.
The day unwinds his hair
and sets out on the open road.
Each day, a new vision,
      clouds and ravines,
          blue wind and buds.

II

Now grasses, blue, green,
jolt us with their reach,
pushing through the leafmold

to tremble with the urgent energy
of their soft
bristling songs.

These grasses beguile the geese
northward, northward.
Now let us rest in their long touch,
let their delight shimmer over us,
until we too unfurl ourselves
through this living world.

Under a blaze of maples,
under birches shaking their catlins,
under white pine's massive buoyancy,
over strawberries ripening,
over these hills echoing
with buds and gusts of rain,
let us walk gratefully in this living
world again.

Breaking Through

Each morning I dig
in sand on the south side of my house.
The knowledge of many hands
guides my hands now
as I pull globs of brassy sweet sand,
shrapnel, bits of crock,
chips of decayed timber up
through ripe damp layers of earth.

While ants bear a procession of crystal children
on their backs,
and beetles scale a lost harvest
of leaves, my knees dampen from earth.
I scoop a place to lie down
and peer into enveloping dark.

This is my treasury.
With one long stare, granite peaks
and green mountainsides ring my heart
with recognition.
Miners lost under mazeways of rock
pat stone, weigh each breath
in their abyss, listening as I do
for whispers of wind to send us
our second chance,
our other lives with wings
or webbing.

Sometime soon, I'll scoop
sand into your backyard
and listen from that larger hole,

for I heard my brother
drumming under roots of mountain pines.
Sometimes I hear him
still crying, still quivering
in the ditch where he died.

"Come back," I holler to him.
His hand, then arm breaks through.
You watch us struggle in turbulent shadow
until I pull him free,
a man of twenty-five with bean-brown eyes
and the chin familiar to my family.

We laugh. We embrace.
We plan to dance this wedge of sundown
into dawn. He says others in the interior
long for us to love them enough to listen.
While the sun chases red light
into leaves, you step from your porch
framed in juniper. You trace the strata
now exposed to air, and want to know
my plans, my destination.

You don't hear nuances of our songs
help replenish the aquifer.
My brother draws me closer to this threshold
that sustains our dreams.
We want you to curl into the darkness
you've denied, the source of signs,
origin of all roots and wanderings.

As we lean in sand
inside this hollow, we hear children
coughing up coal dust and smog.
We see the Yellow River feeding

on silt, while a man in a Mao suit
pedals his heartache over the rutted roads.
Bamboo sighs through the mist above him.

Somewhere in this strata,
refugees wade the Lempa River.
Like Chief Joseph's band, they pray
they can wade across
before gunships blast them
to a different tomorrow.

My brother and I esteem
this hollow, for here oblivion
will begin to branch in a common hope.
My brother will help you understand how
your grandfather is that stone
and we've arrived at Halfway Crossing.
Birches blur to foam, my sandpile
grows transparent as the sea,
shows itself to be no less substance
bound to spirit than my brother
beside me now.

You want to go inside
and flick on the t.v. Someday above its flash,
above my wheeze in damp air, you'll want
to hear water singing its migration.
At that moment I pray you'll
be drawn down, all way round
into the dark circuit that sustains us
where each secret
claims a common tongue.

Morning Talk

—*for Melissa L. Whiteman*

"Hi, guy," said I to a robin
perched on a pole in the middle
of the garden. Pink and yellow
firecracker zinnias, rough green
leaves of broccoli,
and deep red tomatoes on dying stems
frame his still presence.

"I've heard you're not
THE REAL ROBIN. Bird watchers have
agreed," I said. "THE REAL ROBIN
lives in England. They claim
your are misnamed and that we ought
to call you 'a red-breasted thrush'
because you are
indigenous."

He fluffed up. "Am I not
Jis ko ko?" he cried, "that persistent
warrior who carries warmth
northward every spring?"
He seemed so young, his red belly
a bit light and his wings, still
faded brown. He watched me
untangling the hose to water squash.

"Look who's talking!" he chirruped.
"Your people didn't come
from Europe or even India.
The turtles say you're a relative
to red clay on this great island."

Drops of crystal water
sparkled on the squash.

"Indigenous!" he teased
as he flew by.

YOUR FIERCE RESISTANCE

—in memory of Josephine Hill Cote

You left no easy legacy, Aunt Jo.
Grandma doctored you with Latin phrases,
entertaining you with word
and world so you would thrive
like your twin sister, Jane.
She studied a career, stayed the wife
of her Irishman who built
a ranch-style house for her,
her life unfolding
at the recommended pace.

But you
raced your Indian motorcycle
around the reservation.
Pebbles scattering from your starts,
wind in your cropped hair,
you aimed beyond the broken barn,
the washtub spilling sodden corn,
aimed beyond a shack
with snot-nosed babies, crying
for more food.

In the photograph your daughter sent of you
in '37, you wear white pants with wide cuffs
and a shirt with rolled-up sleeves.
Your thin face with large dark eyes is eager
to accelerate into ecstacy.
The large horn between the handlebars
glints like a medallion,
swirling with energies only you have known.

II

In Detroit projects, you struggle with abuse.
When your son, buzzed up on the roof, beats rhythms
like Gene Krupa, the hibiscus in your blood urges
a move to California.

You stopped to see us on your way
when I was twelve. I remember how your laughter
scattered light all through the elms.
After you sat on our porch
with all your dreams zinging around,
my father seemed an arch-conservative,
controlling my relative freedom.
You laughed, looking down our street,
"Dare me once, then watch me go!"
Other relatives said you robbed a bank
and I believed. They said
such spunk meant an early grave. Dad never let me
visit your L. A. digs to hang five
on the beach with my coolest of cousins.

III

Twenty years later, you were the one to show me
how I could cut through the crap of my circumstance
with thought and a fine bladed anger.
You'd snap your eyes and pass me
the smoking sensemillian. "Alcoholics
and addicts—the kindest people I know."
To my twelve year old eyes, you and your sister were
opposites, yet now I know
as twins, you turned around both sides of our oppression,
assimilation and resistance in one blood.
Some said you had Bravado!

Others—machissma!
I call it turtle clan tenacity!
It's been no easy legacy, Aunt Jo.

Each summer you returned
to the reservation. We grew to middle age,
but you moved like an athlete at seventy.
Shaped like a sprite thirteen,
you told us we should swim laps
in the local pool each dawn
and eat raw food,
only raw!

A friend who didn't know you well
bet you in casual conversation you couldn't drive
a doubledecker bus.
You were seventy-two when you applied
and went for training,
laughing as you barreled down the aqueducts
with five other trainees,
testing how to turn that big Los Angeles baby,
how to brake
so old ladies could get off
without having to be gymnasts.

You lost your three brothers,
but missed your twin the most.
To keep in tune with us, you tried new things,
graduating from college to become a journalist-
your essays springing from that fierce resistance
which made you flaunt "Scalp 'em"
on your license plate.
You wanted us to know what you had suffered,
while challenging injustice with your smile.

IV

You met Death by accident one day.
When he broke your hip, he whispered you
were battling cirrhosis. You left
that nursing home before Death
could get you down.

I remember when we walked around
the Oneida powwow. The dancers
spun with colors muted by twilight and we sat
in front of a food stand
with fry bread and coffee. Then
you asked me, "What passes from a mother to her child?"
You shifted your thin body
closer and put your elbows on your knees.
"Its mother's blood. The blood remembers,"
you said, straightening up to look me in the eyes,
snapping them in your teasing way.
"Whatever's lost can often be found."

After you bailed out of the first nursing home,
we didn't know where you had gone,
until your daughter
found you in one that understood
your fierce resistance to indignities.
Now when I wonder what to do,
I ask our blood for answers,
believing in my child's way
you dove into the galaxy and swam an easy lap.
If I ask, an answer comes
from some distant corner of the sky.
Underneath the foam of the Milky Way,
you sparkle in a double star,
still charmed by the ways we need,
yet resist our need to love.
You left no easy legacy, Aunt Jo.

A Presence That Found Me Again, Again

Wild plum red as ever
along the river this summer I fade
from my thirties
Roaring across the flats ten years ago
I caught you glowing
In spite of my spume of road dust
watching me
little sun setting in violet leaves
bell ringing in the sea-green dusk
to one moving without moorings
to one singing as she sank
into dark piny canyons

Wild plum ripe as ever
along the river even then
you invited faith in feeling
offered me a time when the sky gleamed
blue as my first mother's milk
buoyed me over swamp and coulee
like notes of a long lost melody
When I gleaned grief
you another reaper shook your red
skirt in leafy shadows

Wild plum red as ever
hanging on the warm edge of summer wind
the road mica bright
doors of sunlit haze
corn stubble
a gold procession against the shore
like long mornings before grief

I couldn't find my crossing
oaks trembled in their turning
smitten by that second most beautiful being
we call death
I couldn't find half my life
until you held me
a tremulous ripple left

in your branches

and wind just awakening
for his rounds

No Longer

I no longer fear the firestorm despair.
Green earth has coaxed my soul
over a blue bridge of forget-me-nots,
into her hollow of oak leaves, lilies.
Now each creek I cross balances
dark and day as birds give no thought
to each wing's weight, but fly, singing.

I no longer expect the firestorm despair
to sear the ground I grow on.
Horns of sumac have broken my blindness.
Thunder's taste glitters on my lips.
The moon urges my blood root's burgeoning.
Her fierce song cools this light I feed on.
Together we travel this river of fervid stars.

WHEREVER IN WINTER

Wherever in winter you go, child,
I hope our prayers flutter behind you in the wind.
The moon's waxing toward a quarter with Venus
shining to its east. Together
they'll travel this January night, crossing each other
at the horizon in a cold moment before dawn.
By that time, you may be crossing for home.

I've asked each tree,
each tower of steel and glass,
each shrub along the alleys if they've seen you passing by.
Without a word, you disappeared
quickly into these quaking cities.
I wake at four a.m., feeling wind blowing
in every room. No one on earth has yet
helped me understand
this bare sadness rushing through dark halls.
Did my father feel this same anxiety,
staring at the blue of his bedroom
on those nights when the smell
of mud and rain filled me with an energy
I never could deny?

I tell myself stories about the prodigal,
the youthful immortals of Asia,
the restless coyote sniffing a pile of snow and shit.
Tomorrow you'll look
from a window where people rush to work,
and perhaps in that moment find the red road
and a friend.

Someone will surely say that is
her child, I recognize the face, and when they ask,
you'll call. I keep faith that wherever you are,
spirits of this earth and sky keep you aware
of how we are related to everything here.

A Place For Silence

In the park or on the street,
I hear them speaking, "You never saw

her find her keys . . ." "Then to his shock. . ."
I settle on a bench inside this park and feel

hard summer wind push on my left shoulder,
while cottonwoods nearby swish

water into rock. Nowhere in these cities
can I find that great silence

where elemental sounds bring round
my heart. Such silence is the well

where wisdom lives. I try attending
what earth teaches, but planes,

cars, trains engage my anxious space
with the shrill drill of their machines.

I feed my soul with a cricket's loving
bow, with the thrip of a dragonfly's wing,

balancing wave and leaf. Although
they've recorded ocean breakers

and swampy croaks, when wisdom comes,
I swim inside the moment, somehow attuned.

Inside earth's great silence is our future.
We can find it if we listen

the way a caribou hunter pauses on the tundra;
far-off he hears snow inside the moon.

SPEAKING WITH MOTHER

—for Rebecca Belmour

In combers breaking on the shore,
she leaves a line of foam with parting waves.
She's always answered me when I have asked,
although her answers never stay.
She loves a crowded place
and many views. At any water's edge,
I find her scribbling whispers.
"Every action that you take," she says,
"makes a whirlpool. Each blow
and each caress begins a pattern
I expand inside your cells.
Even in your gossamer souls,
you spin my rhythms."

In mountains, her voice sweeps
through every tree. On their bark,
her messages remain,
patterns not copying themselves
exactly. She enjoys transforming
root, worm and human bone. Mother, some
have hurt you with their greed,
with poisons they must make
for yellow ingots. "The greatest arrogance,"
she laughs, "begins when they ignore
what their feelings indicate.
So, I send a rain of rotting fish
or shake my plates to make the girders pop."

Some autumn evening, let's curl up
to watch her change
the hues in moonlit clouds.

Though breath and blood and bone keep
dialogues, oppression
has kinked our thought
so we deny the ways she may respond.
Let's sit in silence on the lawn
while shadows of four crows
sweep across the red-leafed trees. She speaks
in pictures, leading us away from avarice and war.
Those of us who believe
she needs our voices
will be here along the river.

THE POWWOW CROWD

—for Heather R. Whiteman

Punky invisibles dance. Germ, mold
and virus, quark and radical ray
spin in cycles beyond our measure.
Peer at them playing and they
find a Grand Entry song you expected.

Familiar elements dance. Soil
and water, fire, rock and air
flash and glitter without four flags.
Although they're solid to our senses,
their leaping stretches wider than our love.

Plants taught us to dance. Fern
and rush, herb and flower, elm
and moody willow reach subtle rhythms
in the wind, team dancing
with each greening cycle of the earth.

Grouse and trout, bear and human being
dance to endure. The oldest prayer's
a drum we hear in the summer
sunlight. With its beat
we honor the lightning in our blood.

Planets also powwow. Earth and moon,
one in blue fringe, the other, yellow, kick-step
with a clever wobble. Jupiter struts
among his moons while Venus
jingles round in solar wind.

The sun, a fancy dancer, balances,
then swerves his flares on this rim
of whirling stars. Differences delight
him in his timeless trance. Any comet
coming in, he'll bring along.

See the edge of it at midnight?
A skirt woven with multitudes of stars.
Serpent Skirt's harmonic hum
quickens all the dancers, releasing them
from contradictions.

I believe other galaxies join in, until
it's like the powwows down in Stroud. What
are nebulae but smoke drifting from campfires?
The drum is far away, but they sing so loud,
it booms in the center of my chest.

FROM BOAT TO BARNACLE

At first I said,
"Find a ledge on my hull, small drifter,
and bore into my being a toehold."
You were the harmless speck of life
meandering close currents
while I plowed the greater waves
and breached broad crests
in this ceaseless chain of unions called the sea.

Then I fancy we took hold of each other
and you latched on, creating
striped blossoms fluttering
before my sideways glance.
I never conceived you to be
the source of my knowledge
of the sea, filtering first through you
to me. Falling through wave
and rivulet, our common motion across
dimensions brought us closer
until now you flaunt the shape
of my demise.

You latched on, lacking what,
I wonder. From where did the energy come
that feathers the air between us?
You say the sea rolls glass into mist
until the message of distress becomes a Man O' War
of many hues, a bubble dangling its pain down
into the deep. It doesn't matter anymore
which direction the current,
for you hook your blossoms on every wave

and keep, in my lunging and skimming
on this surface, the coil
of my renewal. You are the fiercer
one, although gawkers
would never see how my sails
are shaped by the memory
of your curved body, its rugged
whorls so like the one
who sent you.

NOTES

Pg. 9 - In the "Traditional History," the Six Nations Chiefs related the story of the Peacemaker. A central theme in this story is the power of war to bring grief to both sides of a conflict. Both sides must deal with the clouding of minds and disruption which grief causes. The Peacemaker explained the necessity for restoring the aggrieved into a balanced social order, one which recognizes human dependence upon the natural world. The "Traditional History" relates how the Peacemaker instituted the practice of peacemaking as a continuously renewing process.

Pg. 17 - Although Lucy Lippard's work *Mixed Blessings* contained many astute perceptions in her discussion of indigenous artists' works, I felt the need to respond to her comment about Indians being immigrants from Asia. The Bering Strait theory has been repeatedly questioned and continues to be so. The theory diminishes indigenous peoples' sovereignty, their oral traditions and their presence on this continent.

Pg. 22 - The Lord of the Near and Close, The Mirror That Makes All Things Shine, and Obsidian Butterfly are the names of gods and goddesses in *The Popul Vuh*. Izquic is also a character in this story; she is the daughter of one of the Lords of Death. It is through her act of rebellion that the twin heroes are born again.

Pg. 25 - *Timpsila* is the Lakota word for wild turnip. *Maka Sica* is the Lakota word for the badlands in South Dakota. In the poem, I allude to several confrontations which were detailed in Baptiste's Winter Count. He mentioned the Dog Soldiers who died fighting the cavalry at Ash Hollow and the death of High Back Bone who was one of the first to be shot with a bullet from a long distance. To kill an enemy from a distance was cowardly. This death showed the differences between the code of honor among Plains Indian warriors and the cavalry's code of extermination.

Pg. 27 - *Orenda* is a word I've read in Iroquois scholarship which seems to mean creative power.

Pg. 37 - Malcolm Lowry used the name Robinson for himself in some of his poems. He was addicted to luminol, a depressant. He apparently jumped from the Golden Gate Bridge, but I imagine a different path for him. At one point in my life, his poems helped me to understand the grit it takes to live in oppressive situations.

Pg. 47 - The Loon is a constellation on the edge of the western sky which aided the runners at night when they went with messages from one village to another.

Pg. 47 - The Great Wood is a term found in treaty negotiations. It referred to the vast hardwood forest which once extended from the eastern seacoast to the Mississippi.

Pg. 52 - Traverse de Sioux treaty was signed by the Dakota in Minnesota and the United States. The withholding of annuities guaranteed by the treaty was one of the actions which led to the Dakota Conflict.

Pg. 81 - This poem was written from the experience of standing on the Great Wall and hearing how the five horsemen patrolled for barbarian invaders who blasted through it to invade China.

Pg. 83 - Empress Hsaio-Jui was the second wife of the Ming Emperor Wanli whose elaborate tomb in Xi'an I was fortunate to visit in China. Empress Haiao-Ching was Wanli's first wife. The Emperor partied while the people starved. Although Wanli created a famous bath house for his beloved second wife, even as second Empress, she would never have spoken about the tremendous loss of life and human misery caused in creating these monuments. I imagine she delicately edged in her views as a courtesan.

Pg. 86 - Like the earlier two poems, this one reflects upon the trip to China I took as part of the Sino-American Writers Conference in Chengdu. The xun is a Chinese musical instrument that has a particular melancholy sound.

Pg. 89 - *La guarda barranca* is a bird whose habitat is in the brush of ravines in Central and South America.

Pg. 100 - *Jis ko ko* is the Iroquoian name for Robin. In the story, he is a young warrior who confronts the old man of winter. The old man uses ice and brutal winds to keep *Jis ko ko's* warmth away from the earth. When the old man shoots him on the chest with an arrow of ice, the young man bleeds and transforms into the bird. Even as a bird, he continues his purpose, bringing warm rain and growth—green leaves, flowers and fruit.

Pg. 106 - Bob Brown, an Oneida from the Thames Band who teaches at Oneida, Wisconsin, explained at a gathering once that the Oneida say the Creator gave us two beautiful beings to accompany us in life. The first most beautiful being is life and the second one is death. Working on the poem, I remembered his comment.

Pg. 113 - Rebecca Belmour, an Ojibwa visual artist from Canada, visited St. Paul and brought her large megaphone, part of an exhibit, titled "Speaking To Our Mother." As part of the exhibit, the people who came spoke into the megaphone to the earth. Our voices carried a distance of two miles, into the business district of St. Paul. I wrote the poem after this occasion.

Pg. 116 - Serpent Skirt is the Mayan goddess associated with the galaxy; she resolves all contradictions in her dance. Stroud, Oklahoma has one of the largest powwows I've ever attended. When I was there, it took 3 hours for Grand Entry.

Pg. 117 - I wrote this poem feeling how the large is determined by the small, whether it is a sail boat, catamaran or family relationship. I thought also of D. H. Lawrence's poem, "The Ship of Death," with its admonition that we need to build a ship of death "for the dark flight down oblivion." In this poem, the image of barnacles brought me the feeling that the process of breaking into small forms is not oblivion, "a quietus," but the recognition of mutual interdependence—large and small, spirit and matter.

Roberta Hill Whiteman, an enrolled member of the Oneida Nation of Wisconsin, is a poet, fiction writer and scholar. She is the author of *Star Quilt*, her first collection of poetry. Her recent work has appeared in *The Returning the Gift Anthology; Reinventing the Enemy's Language;* and *Talking Leaves.* An associate professor of English and American Indian Studies at the University of Wisconsin, she has received a Lila Wallace-Reader's Digest Award and a Chancellor's Award from the University of Wisconsin. She is working on various projects, including a biography of Dr. L. Rosa Minoka Hill, the second American Indian woman physician. She is married to Ernest Whiteman who is an Arapahoe sculptor and the illustrator of this collection, and together, they have three children, Jacob, Heather and Missy.